To My Brother in
Christ.
— Ricky Owens —
prophet, father, preacher,
husband, faithful servant
and precious son.

I Love you

{ father of the
fatherless }

1

KNOWING
GOD
AS FATHER

*To My Father God Himself,
I love thy Name, thy Mind,
& thy Heart. Give me thy mind,
heart & ofcourse, thy Spirit,
For Thy Glory, Lord Jesus Christ*

by

JAMES ROBISON

Published by LIFE Outreach International
P.O. Box 982000, Fort Worth, Texas 76182

Editorial Services provided by Wendy Stackable

Cover Design by LIFE Outreach International Graphics Services

ISBN 0-9653940-0-X
Library of Congress Catalog Card Number: 96-094716

Printed in the United States of America.
First Printing: August 1996.
Second Printing: July 2000.
Third Printing: March 2001.

DEDICATED TO...

those who have had no fathers,
who have had absent fathers or
fathers unable to fulfill their role
in the family, and those who have
been blessed with good fathers–in
the hope that, through this book,
the reader might enter into a
joyful, personal relationship with
the ultimate and eternal Father.

You Can Have the Perfect Father

Where is Daddy?

Why won't Daddy play with me more?

Why doesn't Daddy ever talk to me?

Will Daddy be at the game to watch me play?

Why is Daddy so mean to us?

Do I have a Daddy, like other kids?

You may have heard questions like these–perhaps in your own home. If you are like many parentally deprived people, you may remember asking some of those very questions yourself in childhood.

It is a well-known fact, easily proven by statistics, that the role of the father is greatly lacking in North American life. The following incident dramatically illustrates the father crisis in America and its destructive impact on many lives.

Not long ago a chaplain in a federal prison came up with the idea of helping convicts honor their mothers on Mother's Day. A greeting card company furnished Mother's Day cards for the prisoners. All an inmate had to do was pick up a card and mail it to his mother. Almost all of the prisoners responded to the offer. Over 500 inmates requested and mailed the free Mother's Day cards!

Inspired by the success of that project, the chaplain decided to do the same thing for Father's Day. Again, the company furnished the cards, and the prisoners only had to ask for them and mail them. But the result was shockingly different. *Not one inmate requested a Father's Day card for his dad!*

Fortunately, not every man or woman who grows up without a good father lands in jail. But many are scarred for life by the experience. It is such a common problem that, if you have enjoyed a meaningful relationship with your father, you are specially blessed and have much for which you can be thankful.

Did you realize that you can have a relationship with the true God as your own Father?

As for me, I grew up without a father. I was born as a result of a forced sexual relationship when a lust-driven man forced his affections on a woman who served as a practical nurse for his ailing father. The result of that forced sexual encounter was my conception. My mother shared the rest of the story with me when I was in my early teens. After a doctor refused to abort the unwanted child, my mother, not knowing how she could care for me, prayerfully pondered her dilemma. She said God told her that she should have the baby and that her child would bring joy into the world.

My father had no desire whatsoever to be part of my life. He never took me fishing. He never played ball with me. He never said, "That's good, son." His lack of involvement deeply wounded me and created a terrible sense of insecurity, guilt and fear, feelings that handicapped me emotionally for many years. It was only when I met Jesus, and He introduced me to His perfect, heavenly Father, that I was able to overcome the hurts of the past and find real meaning in life.

I am so grateful that although I never had a healthy relationship with my earthly father, I did come to know God as the loving, attentive Father He is. As a result, I have been able to share great joy with many people. I have seen thousands upon thousands come to know God as their Father. This is a most joyful experience–for me as well as those who respond to the truth I share in this book.

Though I was without a father much of my life, I lived in a foster home off and on throughout my youth and later in my teen years. A pastor and his wife gave me a home when I was small. Then my mother took me from that home and I lived with her until I was 15 years old. At that time, I then returned to the pastor and his wife. *During my years with them, I did see the image of a caring father. In the pastor's life, I observed how a father can and should respond to life's situations while interrelating with a child.*

This unofficial "foster dad" made an indelible imprint on my life. I saw the love he had for me, his wife, his own daughter and grandchildren and for all children. The pictures he painted before my eyes were those of care, compassion and genuine interest in the well-being of all with whom he came into contact. *It was because of the influence of this pastor and his wife, and some young people in their church, that I came to know God as my own Father.*

Regardless of our background, circumstances, failures or successes, *each of us has a deep and very real personal need for a relationship with God as Father. He is the one and only perfect Father,* the one from whom all effective fathers must ultimately learn. He is the all-knowing, all-caring, all-sufficient, almighty God. Yet in His written Word, the Bible, God reveals Himself to us as our Father.

Because of Jesus, who has done the most to teach us, we can address this supernatural being as our personal Father. In the model prayer, commonly known as "The Lord's Prayer," He tells us to begin by saying, "Our Father which art in heaven."[1] *The apostle Paul assures us that we can speak to God using the intimate word for "Father," the Greek word "Abba."*[2]

Jesus continually referred to God as His Father. Over and over He stressed that we could know God as our Father, too.[3] Regardless of how great a father we may have on this earth, there is no father like God. Who else has numbered the very hairs on our head? [4] Who else observes every act of our lives with a care so intense that not even a sparrow can fall to the ground without His notice?[5] Jesus pointed out that we are of much greater value than sparrows and assured us that *"if God watches over the birds of the air and all created beings and provides for them all, He is surely much more certain to watch over and provide for us."* [6]

When we discover the possibility of knowing God as Father, a question automatically comes to mind: "How?" *How can we know, in a personal way, this supernatural being who is so powerful?* How can we, mere humans that we are, develop a personal relationship with such a magnificent being?

Well, the Bible tells us. I believe that *the Bible contains God's revelation of Himself to us* and a master plan for abundant, meaningful life, as well as clear directions for receiving eternal life. And in the Bible, we find that the only way to come into a true relationship with God is through a spiritual experience.

Jesus described this experience as the new birth. He said that unless a person is born from above–of the

---

[1]Matthew 6:9 (KJV) [4]Matthew 10:30
[2]Romans 8:15 [5]Matthew 10:29
[3]John 17:24-25 [6]Matthew 10:31

Spirit–he cannot enter the kingdom of Heaven.[7] In other words, without this spiritual experience and encounter with God, you cannot know Him as Father and have the eternal life that it brings–life that assures a never-ending future, as well as the potential for abundant life here and now. [8]

Jesus very specifically delivered this message on the need for a spiritual birth to the most righteous, religious person he ever faced: a Pharisee named Nicodemus. He had to clear the air concerning how one comes into right relationship with God. The people of His day believed they could be accepted by God in only one way–through perfect obedience to all of their religious rules and regulations. *But Jesus revealed that it is not through religious practices, or by doing good works, that we please God.* Rather, He said, it is a matter of accepting God's gift to us.[9] That gift is eternal life–God's kind of life–and we receive it simply by believing in Him and entering into a personal, spiritual relationship with Him.

So, when this religious man called Nicodemus asked the question, "How can a man be born when he is old?" *Jesus explained that, just as we are born physically, we must also be born spiritually.* The Bible reveals that the tremendous need for this new birth was the result of man's sinful nature and sinful behavior.[10] The sinful nature results in deliberate acts of disobedience–doing our own thing, going our own way. *Our sinful nature and sinful behavior have separated us from God.*[11] As a result, we have all gone astray and failed miserably in life. That is why we must be born again–to receive a new nature, one that

---

[7] John 3:3

[8] John 10:10b

[9] Ephesians 2:8-9

[10] Ephesians 2:1-3

[11] Isaiah 59:1-2

comes from a new Father, God, so that we can be changed in what we are and stop our sinful behavior.[12]

Before people will receive this new birth, they must realize that they are sinful and need to be forgiven and changed. *If people do not believe they need to be lifted from defeat and despair, they will never cry out for the help that can only come from above.* Until a person realizes he is drowning, he is not likely to cry for help.

Having come into the world with a sinful nature, we have broken the Ten Commandments.[13] We have had other gods before the one, true God. We have not always honored those we should honor—our parents, for example. We have not been righteous in many areas of our lives, including our thought life.[14] We have a need for cleansing and renewal.

Let me explain with the following illustration the importance of recognizing your need for God's way of life. Imagine boarding an airplane and receiving a parachute from a flight attendant, who says, "Put this parachute on; it is necessary that you wear it." If you were the only one on the plane wearing a parachute, you might be terribly embarrassed, especially if the plane cruised across the United States without incident. Others would be looking at you and asking why you were wearing a parachute. You would feel conspicuous with all that undue attention, and you might even begin asking yourself: "Why am I wearing this parachute? It is limiting me. I look silly!" And before long, most likely, you would take it off. You simply would not be convinced you had a need for it.

But it would be a different story if you knew that,

---

[12] Ezekiel 36:26-27, 2 Corinthians 5:17-18
[13] Exodus 20:2-17
[14] Romans 3:1-12, 23

during the flight, a disaster would occur and the only way for you to escape safely would be by using the parachute. You wouldn't be concerned about criticism, mockery or any assaults intended to embarrass or hurt you. You would rest in peace, knowing you had the way of escape.

In the same way, *we need God as our security, safety and way of escape from separation.* That is an absolute fact![15] Without a proper relationship with God, every one of us is doomed not only to continue repetitious behavior that keeps us in a pit of despair and defeat, but also to be eternally cut off from the very life God so freely offers.

God so loved us that He gave His own Son, Jesus, to take our punishment, our sentence for all the wrong we have done, and to give His life for us.[16] When we realize this wonderful fact and receive this Jesus as our personal Savior, *He becomes not only our way to forgiveness and the way of salvation, but also our way to have God as our Father.*[17] Then it does not matter what skeptics may say, for we know that we have escaped the power of recurring defeat and the eternal separation and darkness for which we were headed. We also have been reconciled or united with God as our Father.

We can enter this relationship with God in only one way: by choosing to take God at His word and to receive the gift He has offered us through the death and resurrection of His own Son, Jesus.[18]

His written Word, the Bible, teaches that Jesus died for our sins, that He paid the penalty for all those sins, that God raised Him from the dead, and He is alive

---

[15] Acts 4:12

[16] John 3:16

[17] John 14:6

[18] John 1:12-13, Romans 6:23

right now![19] And this further miraculous truth: *We can have Jesus living His resurrected life in us in the spirit!*

When we choose to believe this and to accept the gift of life God has given us through His Son, asking Him to forgive our sins and receive us, we immediately receive an eternal grant from God Himself.

Where we deserved death, He gives us life. Where we were in bondage and defeat, He gives us freedom and victory.[20] We become the adopted sons and daughters of God![21]

Jesus said, "No one comes to the Father but through Me."[22] He also said, "I am the way, the truth and the life." What does that mean? First *no one is going anywhere of eternal value and meaning without Him.* Second, there is no real knowledge apart from a relationship with God the Father, who is the fullness of knowledge and wisdom. "I am the LIFE." There is no real life apart from Him–just an empty shell of existence. And, by the way, *emptiness cannot be filled with religious affiliation and activities.* We're talking about RELATIONSHIP, a relationship that is meaningful, life-changing and magnetically attractive to others when they see it.

God says we can be His adopted children.[23] My wife, Betty, and I have two beautiful daughters. What a joy they are! But between those two daughters, we discovered that Betty had a minor medical condition known as endometriosis. Thank God, she was later wonderfully healed by the power of God. But at the time, it seemed unlikely that she would be able to bear another child. So we adopted a son, Randy. We

---

[19] 1 Corinthians 15:2-4   [22] John 14:6
[20] Ephesians 2:5-6   [23] Ephesians 1:4-6
[21] Ephesians 1:5

can honestly say that our love for our son is as great as the love for our biological daughters. It is unique and special. We have shared our total beings with him. What a joy he has been in our lives! When I explained how we adopted him, I used the passages of the Bible where God tells us we have been spiritually adopted as His children. *This is what happens when you come to know God as Father–you are adopted into His family!* And you become an heir to all that God has through Jesus Christ.[24]

You may have been abandoned by your natural parents, or someone may have had to remove you from an abusive situation. But when you are born again, you literally become one of God's sons or daughters! You are given a new identity in Christ. You have a new family that wants you and is willing to nurture you.

God's family is not limited to one household or city or nation. His family of believers reaches across national and racial boundaries, beyond denominations, beyond educational and economic lines to embrace every man, woman and child who acknowledges Jesus as Lord and Savior. What's more, this family was created for the purpose of developing intimacy and trust. In short, the Father's "house" is a safe environment for you! No matter what you have suffered in the past, there are family members waiting to comfort and encourage you and show you more of the Father's love.

I told Randy that he was very special, just as all of us are, because when we receive Christ as our Savior and become Christians, we are adopted as the children

---

[24]Romans 8:16-17

of God. Even as a small boy, Randy understood what I was talking about because he knew our family, as Christians who had accepted the grace of God, had become children of the heavenly Father.

It is difficult to understand how we can be spiritually joined in a genuine relationship with God. We are finite, frail, failing, fleshy beings. He is the infinite, divine, never-failing, supernatural, spiritual Creator God. But we can be joined to Him! And as a matter of fact, *we must be joined to God in order to discover what a wonderful Father He is* and, through that discovery, find the ultimate fulfillment possible in this life and beyond.

I spent much of my time as a little boy wishing I had a dad. Someone to talk to, someone to play catch with, someone to go fishing with. But I didn't have a dad, except for the few years I spent with the pastor. And, oh, what a significant impact the experiences of those years had on my life.

I had at least some idea of what a father should be, because I observed the life of the pastor. I was on his mind, in his heart. He cared enough to give oversight to the things I did. He affirmed me. He approved the things I did. He encouraged me.

When I was very small, I always wanted somebody to watch me and cheer me on as I attempted different boyhood feats. But I didn't hear that encouragement. I didn't receive the approval of a close, caring person when I did well. *Oh, how our hearts long for affirmation, acceptance and approval of a loving father.* All of this God graciously offers. All we must do is accept it by receiving Jesus as Lord, Master and Savior.

I pray that, as I share with you your need to know God as Father, I am able to help you see with eyes of understanding the beauty and joy of the wonderful relationship God has made possible for us to have with Him.

When I was a little boy, I especially wanted my dad to take me fishing. Sometimes I would just sit outside and imagine I was fishing. *I now tell people everywhere I go that my Father, God, takes me fishing. And he knows where the fish are!* Of course, those in the audience smile or laugh. But then I often quickly add that, although He knows where they are, He won't always tell me! He likes to watch me look for them. And, yes, my Father in heaven enjoys my excitement when I do, in fact, catch a big one!

In using such lighthearted illustrations, I am in no way exaggerating the genuineness of the intimacy we can have in our relationship with the Father. As the old hymn says, "He walks with me and He talks with me." *Yes, we can learn to hear His voice and distinguish sounds in the spiritual realm.* God is far more eager to talk to you and me than we ever are to listen.

I have learned that *a true understanding of prayer is not just communicating our heart's desire, our questions and concerns to God. It is also meditating and remaining silent long enough to hear God speak to our heart through His Spirit.* You can understand His voice. Jesus said the people of God know His voice.[25] He pictures Himself as our Savior, as a Shepherd who leads the sheep not only to safety, but also to good pasture, where we receive nourishment.[26]

The Bible is a source of spiritual nourishment.[27] Contrary to impressions some may get, you can

---

[25] John 10:4, 27
[26] John 10:3, 10
[27] Matthew 4:4, 1 Peter 2:2

understand the Bible. It is not nearly as complicated as some theological minds seem to present it and as many in our world system conceive it. *In the Bible He has shown us what He is like through His Son, Jesus, because Jesus Christ is the exact representation of God's nature.* Jesus reveals the Father.[28] In His life, as presented in the Bible, we can see God's love, tenderness and strength; His capacity to inspire and to lead; His willingness to hold, care for, cover and protect us. We see God pictured as a shelter, fortress, mighty rock, foundation, pillar, shield. We see Him as a helmet protecting our thoughts and minds. A breastplate protecting our hearts. A mighty warrior, a strong and conquering lion. And a gentle lamb.

When trying to understand the heart of our Father, *we see Him clearly revealed in the world-famous story known as "The Parable of the Prodigal Son."*[29]

In this story, Jesus tells of a father who had two sons. One of them went to his father, saying: "I want all of my inheritance, and I want it now!" The father in love permitted the son to have his share of the family inheritance. The rebellious lad went into a far country and wasted all his substance and wealth with riotous, selfish, self-centered, wicked living. When he had lost everything he had, he was actually forced to sell himself as a slave in that far country just to survive. The owner and master sent him into the pigpen to feed the hogs. *While in the pigpen, he realized the sorry state that he had reached, how he in foolishness and rebellion had left the security and love of a relationship with his father and had gone out to have his own way in life.*

[28]Hebrews 1:3
[29]Luke 15:11-32

All of us at some point have chosen to take all God has entrusted to us and have done our own thing. Many have wasted their substance in this way. And please understand *that every moment we live outside the will of God and a proper relationship with the Father is wasted.* Believe it when I say the "far country" is one step outside the will of God. The problem has nothing to do with distance. It is simply the matter of our setting out to do our own thing, rather than seeking with all our heart to do the will of God. When we do that, we inevitably find that, as a result of our ways, we are sold out to some system of slavery in this world.

Different ones of us find ourselves enslaved to different things. For one, it may be a habit, attitude or emotional hurt that brings pain and bitterness. For another, it may be an addiction to some substance or an entrapment by some controlling factor.

Whatever it may be, I am glad to announce the good news. When we recognize that we have placed ourselves in bondage and fallen into the resulting pigpen of despair and defeat, *we can do what the prodigal son correctly and wisely did. He got up and went back to the father.*

When he neared his father's home, something truly remarkable happened. He didn't get the angry, scolding reception he probably expected and thought he deserved. His father was watching for him. I believe he looked every day to see if this boy might come down that road. When he finally saw the young man coming, he didn't look the same as he did when he left. Then he was haughty and arrogant, proud and standing tall. Now, coming down the dusty road, he was the figure of one stooped, bent and broken. But the father knew him. It was his boy! And while he was yet a long way off, the father ran to him. And I can promise you, *the minute you turn your heart toward God and head toward your wonderful, loving heavenly Father, He will do more than meet you halfway. He will run as that boy's father did to receive you into His arms.*

This young man is a true picture of repentance. Repentance did not occur when he simply said, "I'm sorry." Repentance did not even occur when he said, "I'm going to get out of the pigpen." The true, life-changing, life-giving repentance occurred when he got up and went back to the father.

We, too, must acknowledge that we have failed. In our heart, mind and spirit and say, "I will go to the Father." And, like that boy who wept out of a broken heart, every one of us should say: "Father, I'm not worthy to be your son. I just want to be a servant." We, too, should acknowledge the fact that we're not worthy of knowing God as Father or the forgiveness that He so freely and fully offers.

But, unworthy as we are, we can know Him, and He wants us to know Him. And no, He doesn't want a slave. He doesn't want a servant. He wants a son. That's what the father said to this boy. He put a ring on his hand, saying, "You are my son." He put a royal robe on him, saying, "You are my son." He put sandals on his feet, saying, "I want you to have peace on your feet, son." And then he killed the fatted calf and threw a "welcome home" party for him.

I can promise you—even at this moment, as you consider turning your life over to God to let Him be to you the Father He so yearns to be—that *all of heaven stands alert, attentive, ready to throw a party in your behalf.* For Jesus Himself said there is rejoicing in heaven over one sinner who repents, one person who says, "I will leave my way and go His way—seeking with all my heart to know God as my Father."[30]

As you come to understand the wonderful truths in much of the Old Testament, you'll see a great story there about King David. You may remember the story of David and Goliath, how the young shepherd boy took his slingshot and killed the giant, the enemy of the nation Israel. David had also killed a bear and a lion while he was a shepherd boy. The bear and the lion were the enemies of the sheep.[31] Goliath was the enemy of the sheep of God–His children, His people–and David killed him.[32]

Later in life, after David became king, he failed morally. Even though he was a king chosen by God, he, too, was defeated by sin. He became momentarily like the prodigal son.

But the beauty of David is this: ***When his sin was called to his attention, David in brokenness said: "I want to know the joy of my Father.*** I want to know that special unbroken relationship, communication and harmony I once had with Him. With all my heart I want it."[33]

David never once, after recognizing and admitting his failure, tried to recapture his kingdom. He didn't attempt to tidy up his public image and make sure that everyone continued to have great admiration and appreciation for him. He never thought about his world at all. He thought only about God's kingdom, God's family, his relationship with his Father. And he pursued those things with everything that was within him. ***He knew the relationship with***

---

[30] Luke 15:10   [33] Psalm 51:6-12
[31] 1 Samuel 17:36
[32] 1 Samuel 17:50

God as Father was more important than being king and having people sing his praises. He knew that relationship was more important than recognition, and he focused all his attention on that one thing.

The Bible says that David was "a man after God's own heart."[34] Many people have misinterpreted this to mean that David's heart was just like the heart of God. But this is not exactly so because God has never failed as David failed. When the Bible says *David was a man after God's own heart,* I firmly believe God is revealing what He desires each one of us to be, and He was saying it in praise of David.

Here is what I think the Bible was saying: That David *was a man in hot pursuit of the heart of God,* and this is what God wants all of us to be. *More than anything, David wanted his heart to be like God's.* It wasn't always so, but, oh, how he longed for it to be! That was the consuming quest of his life, and so it should be with all of us.

I can say by way of personal testimony that I did not have an earthly father to guide and encourage me. But I now have a heavenly Father. Many times I knelt by the bedsides of my children when they were small and literally said to God in a broken and contrite way: "God, I don't know how to be a father. I didn't have a daddy. Please help me be a good father." And *I believe with all my heart God answered and helped me be a loving, caring father.* And I have seen the beauty of His love and life expressed in our children and now our grandchildren.

To say that our children and grandchildren are full of life is a gross understatement. They have a relationship

---

[34] Acts 13:22

22

with the Father–not only the Father of light, but of life. They are full of life! What beautiful pictures! Oh, the joy of seeing children grow up to love God!

Perhaps you have seen your life, your children's lives and the lives of others you love devastated by the effects of sin and the world. It may be that they have not known God and lived for Him with all their heart. If so, *just know that God is big enough to put it all back together.* He's the One who can take the broken pieces of any life and work them together like a puzzle that shapes a beautiful masterpiece, a portrait of joy, peace and meaning. That's what God wants to do for you and your loved ones.

I can honestly say that, although God has blessed me wonderfully, I did fail as a father, *as a man, as a husband, as a person. But my Father in heaven never failed ME.* He never let go of me. He was always eager for me to come back to Him and once again find my way into His arms and discover the fact that I was always in His heart.

And, oh, how He loves me! *He gives me the approval, affirmation and encouragement I have needed since childhood.* Every person, every heart needs this, and God is offering it to every person reading this book.

I think one thing that positively impacted our children more than any other is the fact that *their dad, although not always right, was always in hot pursuit of the heart of God.* Even as I share with you the fact that you can know God as Father, and express my desire to see you know Him that way, I can tell you at this moment that I'm in hot pursuit of God's heart. And the relationship I enjoy with God as Father is indescribable!

From this testimony of mine, you can take heart

concerning a certain doubt that may have entered your mind. *You may be thinking: "I grew up without a real father image in my life. I never knew what it was like to have a good, personal relationship with a father. With such a background, can I ever become a strong, mature Christian?"*

The answer is: "Absolutely." You see, one of the most exciting things about having God as your Father is that He does for you the things you can't do for yourself.[35] And, as you yield to Him and let Him renew and strengthen you in the new life He is giving you, *He will show you what you are capable of doing through faith in Him.* He will affirm you as His child. He will approve and encourage you. All the character defects that mar your life and prevent you from behaving as your heart desires, He will enable you to overcome through your new relationship with Him.

Satan, the world and our former sin nature have left their programming in all of us.[36] Paul called this "the law of sin and death" that lives in our members.[37] It is not what we are, once we receive our new nature from God. But it tugs at us to get us to think and behave as we always did before. In that old programming we may see bondages, weakness in regard to certain temptations, and all kinds of negative feelings–inferiority, insecurity, poor self-esteem, anger, bitterness, worries, doubts and fears.

The Bible says when we see these things operating in us, after we receive Christ and have God as our Father, it is no longer us doing them but the sin living in our members.[38] And there is no condemnation for

---

[35] Philippians 1:6, 2:13   [38] Romans 7:17
[36] Ephesians 2:2
[37] Romans 7:23

it, when you have believed in Jesus and you are "in Christ Jesus."[39] However, it also says that *God had provided a way for us to overcome these destructive factors and live lives that are fulfilling to us and pleasing to God.* And that is through the "Spirit of life in Christ Jesus."[40]

And what does "the Spirit of life in Christ Jesus" mean? It means that, when we believe in Jesus and receive Him as Savior, *we have Him living in us by His Spirit.* We can trust in His power to overcome that old programming, that law of sin and death. And, by yielding to Him moment-by-moment in life, we can put to death the things Satan planted in us to steal from us and to kill and destroy us.[41]

Please do not think that, because you have never known a good relationship with an earthly father, you cannot have a good relationship with your heavenly Father. *He will strengthen you. He will help you.* He will uphold you with the right hand of His righteousness[42]–and that right hand is none other than the life of Jesus, His Son, who will live in you by His Holy Spirit.[43]

If you are now ready to consider seeking God as your Father, you need only do what the prodigal son did in the story Jesus told.

You can say, as that son did: "I should have never done it my way, but I have. I have sold out in areas of my life to influences I should never have sold out to and I, too, find myself in bondage, enslaved, entangled and defeated. And I'm willing to admit it. *I need to get up out of the mess I'm in and call it what it is. It is sin.* Certainly, I've sinned in breaking

---

[39] Romans 8:1
[40] Romans 8:2-4
[41] Romans 8:13

[42] Isaiah 41:10
[43] John 14:16-17, 1 Corinthians 3:16

the first commandment, 'Thou shalt have no other gods before Me,' because I've had other gods before the real, living God, who wants to be my Father. I admit it, and I want to be forgiven. I have done it *my way* long enough–now I want to do it *God's way.* "

After saying that, **you must be willing to do as that prodigal son did: He left the self-centered way of life** he had followed, along with the defeat, despair and filth that resulted from it, and **he headed for the Father.**

If you, in this moment, will say: "Father, I'm headed straight for You. With all my heart, I want You to accept me; I want You to receive me. I give myself to You. That's what I want." If you will do that, you will know Him as Father. **He will show you how, through belief in Jesus Christ, to be born again and become His child.** Yes, God in heaven will be your Father through faith in Jesus Christ.

The following story should touch your heart while illustrating what it means to commit to God as your Father.

Years ago, a writer while chatting one day with a minister said: "Preacher, you are famous for preaching Jesus. That's all you talk about–Jesus."

"Thank you," the preacher said. "I'm glad to be known as a preacher who talks about Jesus."

"Well, sir," the man said, "could I tell you my story about Jesus?"

And the preacher said: "Certainly. I'll listen to anything you care to tell me about Jesus, my Savior."

And so the writer told him this story:

I was an agnostic. To be very honest with you, I hated God. I hated Him so much that I would never let my wife or anyone in my family mention the name of God in my presence. As a matter of fact, I never let anyone in my family go to church if I knew they were going in time to stop them. That's how I was.

Then one day I was sitting upstairs in my study writing when, suddenly, I heard a commotion downstairs. I rushed down, pushed open the front door and saw a stranger in front of the gate that opened onto the street. A twisted, bloody bicycle lay on the steps behind him.

"Whose bicycle is this?" I shouted at the man as he turned to walk up the street. And the man said, "Sir, that's your boy's bike."

I said: "Where is my boy?"

"I don't know where he is," the man said. "They took him away in an ambulance, and I don't know where they took him."

Running back inside, I began to call every hospital in the area. Finally, I found a hospital that had just received an injured boy in the emergency room. I drove to the hospital, and when I walked into the emergency room, I saw a hand lifted up from a stretcher bed. It was my son, little Bill, raising his hand.

I rushed over to him and said, "Son, son, you are going to be all right." My little boy clutched his fingers and began to talk to me.

"Daddy," he said, "I've really been hurting. I've been hurt real bad and, you know something? When I was lying out there in the street, I was all by myself. There wasn't anybody there, Daddy–not anybody. But you know something? While I was lying there, I remembered one day when you didn't know about it, and I went to Sunday school and church. In Sunday school, a lady told me that if I ever got into trouble, or if I ever got hurt, or if I ever needed a friend, Jesus was the best friend a boy could ever have.

"So, Daddy," my son said, "right there in the street, I prayed. I prayed to Jesus. And you know something. I'm almost glad to go."

I said, "Son, you are not going anywhere; you are going to be all right, son."

But he said: "No, Daddy, I'm going to die, but it's all right. It really is. Daddy, would you pray with me right now?"

I said, "Son, don't ask me to pray; I've never prayed, son, and I don't know how."

And he said, "Daddy, I'll tell you what the teacher told me, and you can just say that."

"No, son, I can't."

"Please, Daddy, just for me, please."

Finally, I said, "All right, son," and as I bowed my stubborn head, I heard my little boy say:

"Our Father which art in heaven..." and I repeated it after him.

"Hallowed be Thy name..." and I said that after him.

"Thy kingdom come..." and I repeated that.

***"Thy will be done**...," I could not say it!*

*His fingers tightened their grip on my hands, and he said: **"That's it, that's it. Say that, Daddy—say it and mean it, please, Daddy, please!"***

Once again, I bowed my head and prayed, "Thy will be done."

Suddenly, his little hand fell limp in mine. I looked up to see eyes that were set, lips that were fixed, never to smile again.

Preacher, my little son was gone. He was gone, preacher. But—miracle of all miracles, marvel of all marvels—the Jesus that went away with my little son stayed in my heart, Lord and Savior forever and ever. That's my story about Jesus.

What God did for that father in that moment and forever He wants to do for you and every person.

Would you right now bow your head and say, *"Thy will be done"?* And we know it's God's will for you to receive Jesus as Savior and Lord. Would you say: "Jesus, I do believe You died for me and gave your life for my sin. I acknowledge I have sinned, and I receive You as my only source of salvation. I receive You as my Lord, my Master and my Savior. I want to know God as my Father. Come into my life, Lord Jesus,[44] and, *Lord God, become my Father just as You are the Father of Jesus.* With all my heart I want to pursue You and know your heart. In Jesus' name I pray."

[44] Revelation 3:20

PART II

Getting to Know Your Heavenly Father

If you have prayed to receive Jesus Christ and invited Him to be your Lord and Savior, whether just now or at some earlier time, you have become a child of God. You have a new Father, and He is none other than the almighty God, the Creator of the universe!

Because of His majestic greatness, your first impulse may be to draw back in awe, to fear Him and to worship Him from afar. But that is not the kind of relationship your new Father wants with you.

"God is love," the Bible says, and "perfect love casts out fear" (1 John 4:16, 18). It also says those who abide in love abide in God, and He in them.

God doesn't want you to be afraid of Him. He is a loving Father, and He wants you to draw near to Him and get to know Him in the most personal, intimate way—in exactly the way a kind, loving earthly father would want to know and be known by a treasured son or daughter. In Galatians 4:9, we are told: "But now that you have come to know God, or rather to be known by God..."

Throughout the Bible, God emphasizes that this is what He desires most—to know His children in an intimate, personal way and to be known by them. In Jeremiah 8:2, He complained because "those who handle the law did not know Me." He had the prophet Hosea plead, "So let us know, let us press on to know the Lord" (Hosea 6:3). And through the same prophet, He let it be known that *He preferred for His people to seek to know Him rather than to spend their lives in sacrificial service to Him.* "For I delight in loyalty rather than sacrifice. And in the knowledge of God rather than burnt offerings" (Hosea 6:6).

The apostle Paul heard these words loud and clear. And, once he had experienced the love and majestic presence of Jesus, who is the exact likeness of God, he gave up everything in order that he might get to know Him fully (Philippians 3:7-10).

I urge you, like Paul, *to make a lifetime commitment to seek with all your heart to know this new, loving Father of yours.* He will reveal Himself to you in many ways: Through everyday experiences of life, through nature, through the lives of other people who know Him. Through words, God speaks through the Holy Spirit directly to your spirit.

But by far, His most effective way of letting you get to know Him is through His written Word, the Bible. The following study will help you understand better the new, spiritual birth you have just received in trusting Jesus as your Savior. But it is designed primarily *to lead you into the exciting lifelong practice of getting to know the Father by searching the Scriptures.*

May your new Father make His face to shine upon you as you complete this study. You will come to know personally what it is to be approved, affirmed and encouraged by your Father in heaven. Upon this reality you can build the most meaningful life possible.

Suggestions for Learning Faster

No doubt you want to learn about your heavenly Father and your relationship with Him as rapidly as you possibly can. Let me offer these suggestions to help you learn faster.

1. Use the Bible. As you read through this book, have a copy of the Bible handy. I pray that the thoughts I share will inform, inspire and encourage you. But there is power in the written Word of God, the Bible. It is more than just words. It is God speaking directly to you. The Holy Spirit will bring it to life to you, so that it will become the living Word of God to you. To help your understanding, I suggest a modern translation. The verses I quote in this book are from the New American Standard Bible, which is my favorite translation.

2. Take notes. Along with your Bible, bring a note pad and a pen or pencil. As you read from the book and your Bible and the Holy Spirit brings thoughts to mind, jot them down. This will help you understand and remember what you have seen. Also, you will have the notes to review later and to share with others.

3. Focus on the Father. Let forming a relationship with your heavenly Father be your goal. The object of your study should not simply be getting to know more facts, but getting to know a Person, your heavenly Father, and your relationship with Him. God bless you as you begin this exciting spiritual adventure.

Receiving God as Father Through Faith in Jesus

In setting out to know God as Father, it is best to start with an understanding of all that is involved in receiving Him as your Father. You need the answers to questions like these:

Why did I need God as my Father to begin with?

What did God do to become my Father?

What incredible gift did God give me through Jesus?

What did I have to do to become a child of God?

Having a firm grip on the answers to these questions will give you a good foundation for knowing God as your Father. It will **help you appreciate, more deeply than ever before, the price God paid to have you as His child.** Fully realizing this, you will begin to see His great love for you—and you will be able to love Him more.

The Need for God
As Your Father

Romans 3:23
For all have sinned and fall short of the glory of God.

When you ponder the question "Why did I need God as my Father?" it might help to think first about what a physical father is. A physical father is one who passes his physical life along to his children. That's why children resemble their fathers in appearance. They have received their father's "genetic code" and so, physically speaking, they are like him. They possess his physical nature.

The same thing happens in the spiritual realm. Spiritually, **we all come into the world with a nature passed down through the ages from the first man, Adam.** He was created in the image of God and placed in the Garden of Eden. But he chose to disobey God and become an independent being.

When Adam rebelled against God, he died spiritually. Instead of the nature God intended him to have, he received a sinful nature. **Because he became a sinner in what he was, he was a sinner in what he did.** And Romans 3:23 tells us how that impacted all of our lives. Because we came into the world with Adam's sin nature, we all sinned and came short of the glory of God!

What do the following verses tell you concerning why you needed God as your Father? Romans 3:23, Romans 3:10-18, Ephesians 2:1-3, Romans 6:23a, Ezekiel 18:4

_____

_____

_____

Consider the thoughts you received from the above verses. Which thoughts helped you most to understand your need for God as your Father?

By becoming your Father, God gives you a new nature–His divine nature (see 2 Peter 1:4). In so doing, He changes what you are. How should this change make a difference in what you do?

What God Did to Become Your Father

1. God Sent Jesus, His Only Begotten Son, to Die for Us

Romans 3:24

Being justified as a gift by His grace through the redemption which is in Christ Jesus.

To become your Father, God first had to deal with the legal problem brought on by the sin in your life. As you saw in the previous section, **you deserved the spiritual death penalty for those sins.** Humanly speaking, **there was no way you could avoid this penalty.** You couldn't pay it–except by death. And, since "all have sinned," no one else could pay it for you.

But God loved us so much that He sent His only Son into the world as a man–the only man without sin. And **because He had no sin of His own to pay for, He could pay the penalty for all our sins.** He did so by allowing Himself to be crucified.

Romans 3:24 says we have been "justified as a gift by His grace through the redemption which is in Christ Jesus." **Redemption means Christ paid the price for us to be set free from the death sentence** we had received for our sins. Being "justified" is to be made "just as if you had never sinned."

What fact does each of these verses reveal about what God did to become your Father? Romans 3:24, John 3:16, Romans 5:8, 1 Corinthians 15:3-4, Ephesians 5:2, 1 Peter 3:18

Which thoughts gleaned from these verses make you feel the most thankful to God?

Which verses help you the most to see the love of a Father in God?

2. God Gave Us a New Life Through Jesus

Romans 6:4

Therefore we have been buried with Him through baptism into death, in order that as Christ was raised from the dead through the glory of the Father, so we too might walk in newness of life.

You have seen how God took care of the death penalty brought on by your sins. But to become your Father, God had to do more than just pay the debt for your sins. Remember what we learned earlier about the sin nature we had when we were born physically into the world? Well, **God had to do something about that sin nature,** too. Simply paying for our sin would not give us His spiritual likeness. And **to really be His children, we have to be like Him by nature–in what we are.**

It is impossible with human wisdom to understand how God took away that old sin nature and gave us His divine nature. **But He did so by making us one with Jesus Christ when He was crucified.** He placed your sin nature in Him; and when He died, that "Old Man" died with Him. It was buried with Him. Then, when He was raised, you were raised with Him to share His new resurrection life.

Being changed in what we are doesn't mean that we are changed instantly in all that we do. We CAN still sin. But here's the good news: We can also NOT sin. We are no longer slaves to sin. We can now yield our lives to God as His instruments. And, though we may sin from time to time, we don't have to let any sin dominate our lives. Under grace, we have a new nature. And sin no longer rules over us because, in this new nature, we have God working in and through us to deliver us from the power of sin.

In each of these Scripture passages, you will find truth about the gift of new life God has given you. Romans 6:2-7, Galatians 2:20, Romans 6:23b, Ephesians 2:8-9, Romans 5:10, 2 Peter 1:4, 1 John 5:11, Ezekiel 36:26

Which truths mean the most to you? Why are they so important to you?

Children in the world watch and learn from their earthly fathers. Can you watch and learn from your spiritual Father? If so, how?

Can you still sin, even with God as your Father? (1 John 1:8)

What does God promise, if you do sin? (1 John 1:9, 2:1-2)

Knowing God as Father, what are you able to do? (1 John 2:3)

How Does a Person Receive God as Father?

Romans 10:9-10

That if you confess with your mouth Jesus {as} Lord, and believe in your heart that God raised Him from the dead, you shall be saved; for with the heart man believes, resulting in righteousness, and with the mouth he confesses, resulting in salvation.

You have now heard the answer to two important questions: Why you need God as your Father and what God has done to become your Father. Now we come to the most important question of all: ***How does one receive God as Father?***

Christians can actually be born again and have God as their Father and still not know the true answer to this question. And as a result, they live in confusion, frustration and failure.

It is not the fault of newborn baby Christians that they don't get the right answer regarding how one receives Christ. They are often taught by people who don't know the answer themselves. The wrong answers commonly involve some kind of rules, regulations or works. ***To be saved, new Christians are told they have to abide by certain rules and do certain works and thus earn God's acceptance. But this is not what the Bible says.*** In verse after verse, it follows the theme stated in Ephesians 2:8-9: Salvation is by grace, through faith, and not of works.

Romans 10:9-10, 13 states it very simply: "If you confess with your mouth Jesus as Lord, and believe in your heart that God raised Him from the dead, you shall be saved; for with the heart man believes, resulting in righteousness, and with the mouth he confesses, resulting in salvation...for 'Whoever will call upon the name of the Lord will be saved.'"

Continue learning about your relationship with the Father by reading the following verses. Each contains key action words that will help you understand what a person must do to receive God as Father.

See how many of these key words you can find. Romans 10:9-10, 13, John 3:3, John 1:12-13, John 5:24, Acts 16:31, Revelation 3:20

If you prayed the prayer suggested in Part I, think about what you prayed. *Did you believe in Jesus Christ as the Son of God who died and rose for you? Did you receive Him as your Lord and Savior?* If so, you have done all that the above words suggest to receive God as your Father.

If you didn't pray, or you are not sure *what* you prayed, you may now know more about how to pray. In that case, *you can pray right now, based on what the above verses say, and God will become your heavenly Father.* You can also share with others the need and opportunity they have for receiving Jesus as Lord and Savior.

In Revelation 3:20, Jesus says He will come in and dine with those who open their hearts to Him. What do you think He means in asking us to dine with Him?

Know God as Your Father–
Yourself as His Child

1 John 3:1-2
See how great a love the Father has bestowed upon us, that we should be called children of God; and {such} we are. For this reason the world does not know us, because it did not know Him. Beloved, now we are children of God, and it has not appeared as yet what we shall be. We know that, when He appears, we shall be like Him, because we shall see Him just as He is.

When you received God as your Father, you entered into a relationship with Him. ***Like any relationship, this one is a two-way street. Not only is God your Father, but you are His child.***

Actually, it may be hard for you to think of God as your Father until you have begun to think of yourself as His child. God knows this to be true. As a result, He has placed many verses in His Word to remind us that we are His children and to help us become settled down and live in that wonderful truth.

In 1 John 3:1-2, the Bible tells you in plain words that you are a child of God if you have believed in Jesus as your Savior: "See how great a love the Father has bestowed upon us, that we should be called children of God...Beloved, now we are children of God, and it has not appeared as yet what we shall be. We know that, when He appears, we shall be like Him, because we shall see Him just as He is."

These verses don't merely proclaim that you are a child of God. They point out the exciting way in which that truth will be confirmed when Jesus appears on the earth again. You will see that you are like Him! Think about that. How does this help you realize that you are truly a child of God and that He is indeed your Father?

Let these verses help you see for yourself, even now, what it means to be a child of God. 1 John 3:1-2, Romans 8:16, Galatians 4:6

Prayer was defined in Part I as simply talking to God and letting Him talk to you. In Mark 14:36, Someone uses "Abba" in speaking to God. "Abba" is a familiar name for "father"—like "Daddy" or "Papa" in English. Who was this Person?

What name can you use in talking to your heavenly Father, according to one of the verses above? And what does this tell you about the kind of relationship you can have with your Father?

What benefits come with being a child of God, according to the following verses? Romans 8:17, 1 Peter 1:3-5, 2 Peter 1:3, Hebrews 4:16

Matthew 5-7 contains Jesus' "Sermon on the Mount." In this lengthy passage, count the times Jesus refers to God as "your Father." What does this tell you about who you are and what your relationship is to God?

Know God as:
A Loving Father

Psalm 32:10
Many are the sorrows of the wicked; but he who trusts in the Lord, loving kindness shall surround him.

Many people never experience a real relationship with their natural father. With some, it is because the father does not live in their home. Many others have fathers who live in their home but, for one reason or another, either cannot or will not show affection for their children. As a result, ***many people never feel a father's love.***

I know firsthand how tragic it can be to miss out on the love of a father as you are growing up. It leaves never-healing scars in the lives of some people. Only because I found God as my Father in my late teens did I escape the tragic impact of not having a loving father during most of my childhood.

But ever since I received Jesus Christ as my Savior and came to know God as my real Father, He has been showing me what a wonderful, loving Father He is. In fact, ***I've found that one of the most exciting things about the Christian life is discovering day by day just how much your heavenly Father loves you!***

It doesn't matter how deeply you may have been wounded emotionally and psychologically by not receiving the love you needed from an earthly father. The unfathomable and everlasting love of God can make up for all you missed. ***His love can heal all your wounds*** and remove all your scars. As it fills and pours out of your heart, it can enable you to forgive and love others, just as He forgives and loves you!

The following verses will help you know and understand your Father's love.

See how many different thoughts you can find in them concerning the love of God. Jeremiah 31:3, John 17:23, John 16:27, 1 John 4:10, Ephesians 3:17-19

Which of these thoughts impress you the most? Why?

How will learning and experiencing the love of your heavenly Father affect your life from now on?

Do you feel led to do anything because of your Father's love for you? What, specifically, do you feel led to do? When will you do it?

An Attentive Father

Psalm 139:16-18a
Thine eyes have seen my unformed substance; and in Thy book they were all written, the days that were ordained {for me}, when as yet there was not one of them. How precious also are Thy thoughts to me, O God! How vast is the sum of them! If I should count them, they would outnumber the sand....

"Look, Daddy, look. Look, Daddy, look." If you are a father, you have probably heard those words countless times. If you had a father in the home as you were growing up, more than likely you said those words many times yourself. If you had no father growing up, you longed to have a dad you could call on when you needed or wanted attention. ***Even the best earthly fathers can hardly give their children the time and attention they should have.*** Fathers are busy people. They have to work hard to support their families. When they are not working, they need time for recreation and relaxation. They can't focus on their children every minute they are at home.

But this is not true of your heavenly Father. He is not bound by the physical limitations of an earthly father. He can focus on you every minute of the day and through the night. And He does!

Think what a blessing it is to know that ***your heavenly Father's eyes never leave you.*** You never had to call to Him, "Look, Abba–did you see that?" He was looking. And, yes, He saw it.

The following verses will help you realize just what an attentive Father you have in God. Each of these verses contains truths that show how attentive God is toward His children. By finding these truths, you will be more confident that your heavenly Father is watching over you. Psalm 40:5, Psalm 33:13-15, 2 Chronicles 16:9, Job 24:23, Job 34:21, 1 Peter 3:12

Think for a moment about the truths you just discovered. What does each of them tell you about your Father and your relationship with Him?

How will your attitudes and actions toward God change because of these truths?

How will these truths affect your attitudes and actions toward other people with whom you are in contact?

A Compassionate Father

Psalm 103:13
Just as a father has compassion on his children, so the Lord has compassion on those who fear Him.

A friend told me he witnessed this incident at a Little League baseball game. Having been around these games a lot myself, I can believe it. The kid at bat swings and misses the ball. From the stands, a big voice booms out: "Come on, keep your eye on the ball!" Nothing wrong with the words, but the tone is one of disgust. The kid swings and misses again. This time the voice yells: ***"Keep your eye on the ball, stupid!"*** The man behind that ugly voice is the boy's dad. You can guess the results of his scolding. The boy swung again and struck out.

The young man didn't need a tongue-lashing. He certainly didn't need to be humiliated by his own father. What he needed more than anything was a little compassion. He knew he was performing poorly. His failure–right there for all the teammates, coaches and parents to see–must have been terribly embarrassing. But all he hears is the word "stupid"— and that from the one person in the whole crowd whom he wants most to please!

Our heavenly Father always looks on us with compassion. That word is composed of two words, meaning to "feel with." It carries with it the idea of understanding, as well as love. You can always be sure, whatever difficulty you are facing, that ***your heavenly Father has compassion on you. He understands. He loves you.*** He feels what you feel— your pain, your grief, your sorrow. Now let the Bible show you more about His compassion.

What does each of these verses say to you about the compassion of your heavenly Father? Exodus 33:19, Deuteronomy 32:6, Psalm 40:11, Psalm 51:1, Psalm 72:13, Isaiah 54:10, Joel 2:13, James 5:11

On the basis of the way you have lived and the things you have done, do you feel that you deserve God's compassion?

Why do you think God has compassion for you?

Does knowing your Father's compassion for you in any way change the way you feel toward other people?

A Forgiving Father

Colossians 2:13

And when you were dead in your transgressions and the uncircumcision of your flesh, He made you alive together with Him, having forgiven us all our transgressions.

If you had a natural father, was he forgiving? As a minister, I see many people who have been deeply wounded because their father would not or could not bring himself to forgive them for something they did.

When a person doesn't have a forgiving heart— given to them by God–they can refuse to forgive and carry a grudge for a lifetime. You might understand a father having difficulty forgiving some things–a son or daughter hurting their mother, stealing from the family, becoming involved in crime and bringing disgrace on the father and the family. But, with an unforgiving heart, the offense doesn't have to be a shameful act. It can be not choosing the profession the dad wanted his child to pursue, failing to make the football team, marrying someone the father didn't like. Such feelings of bitterness, resentment and unforgiveness may be understandable in certain circumstances. They may even seem justifiable, but these emotions are damaging to everyone in the family. That's why forgiveness is so important. It opens the door to healing and restoration. But without God's help, real forgiveness is impossible.

Your heavenly Father has a forgiving heart. When He sent Jesus to die for your sins, He made it possible to forgive and pardon you for even the worst offenses without committing an injustice. Jesus has already paid with His blood for all our sins.

Look for your Father's forgiving heart in the following verses. Each of these verses allows us to see God's forgiving heart from different points of view. See how many facts you can learn from them about your Father's forgiveness. Psalm 103:10, Jeremiah 31:34, Psalm 32:5, Psalm 86:5, Ephesians 4:32, Hebrews 8:12, Hebrews 10:17, 1 John 1:19, 1 John 2:12

God's forgiveness is "free" to us because Jesus has paid the debt. However, God asks us to do one thing in order to receive His forgiveness. Proverbs 28:13 tells what that one thing is. Which of the two verses above also mentions this action?

According to Matthew 6:12, 14-15, there is something that could prevent our heavenly Father from forgiving us. Ephesians 4:32 also refers to it. What is it?

Does learning about God's forgiving heart toward you help you know Him better as Father? Explain how.

What changes do you feel led to make in your attitudes toward others, now that you know God as a forgiving Father?

Know God as Your Life Source

Acts 17:28a
For in Him we live and move and exist...

Most people know that their earthly father has given them their physical life. They know they could not have come into the world without a father, although they may never have seen or known the man who is their father. I didn't see my human father until I was a teenager. Still, I knew I had a father who had given me my physical life.

But I wonder how many people—even Christians—fully realize that their real life comes from God. I am talking about eternal life. Life that never ends. Life that can be experienced right now in all its fullness and abundance by everyone who has been born from above.

In Him we live and move and have our existence, the Bible says in Acts 17:28. Apart from Him we would not have life—because there is no life apart from Him.

In Ephesians 2:1, a verse we talked about earlier, we are told that we are dead in our sins before we received Jesus as Savior. We were dead spiritually. **But our heavenly Father has brought us to life spiritually. And spiritual life is what really counts.** Physical life always ends in death, but spiritual life goes on forever.

You will rejoice as you see what all the following verses have to say about your heavenly Father as your source of life.

These Scripture verses share many thoughts about your heavenly Father as the source of your life. Let them bless you by finding as many of these truths as you can. Genesis 2:7, Job 33:4, Isaiah 42:5, John 5:21 and 26, John 6:33, 35 and 63, John 11:25, John 14:6, John 20:31, Romans 4:17, 2 Corinthians 5:17-18, 1 Timothy 6:13

In Matthew 10:1 and 8, Jesus is giving instructions to His followers. What does He say they can do because they have "freely received" life from Him?

Will you choose to believe you can pass spiritual life on to others because you have received your Father's life through Jesus?

Know God as Your Provider

Matthew 6:31-33
*Do not be anxious then, saying, "What shall we eat?"
or "What shall we drink?" or "With what shall we
clothe ourselves?" For all these things the Gentiles
eagerly seek; for your heavenly Father knows that
you need all these things.*

Have you ever stopped to think what a difference it
would make in the world if everyone knew God as
their Father–and Provider? People scheme and strive,
fight and claw to get the basic things they need for
life–things like food, clothing and shelter.

Greed drives many people to cheat, rob and steal
even when they have all the material things they
need. But what is behind that greed? Most likely, it's
a fear of not having enough. They go on scratching for
more and more because, **depending on their own
ability to provide, they can never feel secure with
what they have.**

Jesus tells us that, with our Father as our Provider,
we are set free from this struggle for survival. He says
we are **to seek the Kingdom of God and His righteousness, and everything we need will be added to
our lives.** If people would obey this and believe in
Him, they could live in peace with one another.

Come to know your heavenly Father better as your
Provider in the verses that follow.

What do these verses tell you about God as your
Provider? Genesis 1:29, Exodus 16:8, Deuteronomy
28:8, Psalm 84:11, Psalm 145:16, Psalm 146:7,
Ecclesiastes 5:19, Jeremiah 5:24, Philippians 4:19

Which of the truths learned in the above verses help you the most to have confidence in God as your Provider?

How will knowing God your Father as Provider make a difference in how you relate to other people?

Know God as Your Protector

Isaiah 54:17
"No weapon that is formed against you shall prosper; and every tongue that accuses you in judgment you will condemn. This is the heritage of the servants of the Lord, and their vindication is from Me," declares the Lord.

Since you received Jesus as Savior and started getting to know God as your Father, you may have experienced some unexpected problems. Some of your circumstances may seem to have gone haywire. You may have run into opposition from people you thought were on your side. In other words, you may feel that you have been attacked.

If this sort of thing is happening to you, **don't be alarmed or discouraged.** And if they are not happening, don't be smug–because sooner or later they will come upon you.

What does all this mean? **Simply that when you become a child of God, you become involved in a spiritual battle.** All of God's wicked enemies are now your enemies, too.

And they are out to destroy you because you have become a threat to their evil empire.

Jesus warned us that those who hate Him will hate us (John 15:18-19). But God promises in Isaiah 54:17 that "no weapon formed against you" by any of your enemies will succeed because He will protect you. As you continue, you will find much more comforting truth about your Father's role as your Protector.

In these verses, single out as many thoughts as you can about your Father's commitment to be your

Protector. Exodus 13:21, Exodus 23:20 and 27, Exodus 34:24, Deuteronomy 3:28, Deuteronomy 7:24, Psalm 18:1-3, Psalm 121:5-8, Isaiah 43:2, Isaiah 52:12, Romans 8:31 and 38-39

Which of these thoughts about the protection promised by your Father give you the most comfort?

How will knowing about your Father's protection change the way you think about the problems you are facing?

How will your Father's protection change your attitudes toward other people who may seem to be "the enemy?"

Know God as Your Deliverer

Psalm 34:19
Many are the afflictions of the righteous; but the Lord delivers him out of them all.

In my book, *"Thank God, I'm Free!,"* I tell about the stronghold of lust that I struggled with at the height of my ministry as a crusade evangelist. I was sharing with tens of thousands of people how the truth will make you free, yet I was a captive, defeated in my thoughts and desires. I hated the problem. *I hated the guilt and misery it was bringing down on me and what it was doing to my ministry. But I couldn't overcome it.* It was like a claw that had fastened itself on my brain and refused to let go.

But God sent His deliverance to me. It came not through some visible Christian leader, but through a simple layman–a carpet cleaner with only an eighth-grade education! That man prayed over me in the power of the Holy Spirit, and God set me free.

In the spiritual wars you face daily, the enemy sets all kinds of traps for you. They may take the form of addictions, destructive patterns of thought and behavior, scheming people or the unseen agents and powers of darkness. But whatever they are, your Father promises to deliver you. The verses that follow will give you more exciting assurances that your heavenly Father is both willing and able to deliver you.

Point out as many thoughts as you can from the following verses that help assure you that your Father is your Deliverer. 1 Timothy 1:15, Job 5:19, Psalm 18:16-17, Psalm 40:2, Psalm 41:1, Psalm 91:1-4,

Psalm 118:5-7, Psalm 144:2, Jeremiah 39:17, 2 Corinthians 1:8-10, 2 Timothy 4:18

According to these verses, what are some things your Father promises to deliver you from?

Can you think of some things that your Father has already delivered you from?

How will knowing God as your Father and Deliverer make a difference in the way you deal with bad habits and other traps the enemy sets for you?

Know God as Your Teacher

Psalm 32:8
I will instruct you and teach in the way which you should go; I will counsel you with My eye upon you.

Often in my ministry, I hear Christians exclaim–after surrendering their lives fully to Jesus— "Wow! I got a brand new Bible!" They don't mean they bought a new book. They mean that the Bible, which never made sense to them before, has suddenly sprung to life for them.

You may be able to relate to this experience. *Before we are born again, we don't have the spiritual eyes and the spiritual mind to see and understand the Word of God. But new eyes and a new mind are part of the package we get with our new life when we receive Christ as Savior.*

First Corinthians 2:12-14 points out that the natural man can't understand the things of God. But now that we have received the Spirit that is from God, He reveals spiritual truth to us.

Even since you first began this study, your Teacher-Father may have given new meaning to things that were a mystery to you before. I hope so. But if you are still puzzled about many things, don't be alarmed. *Your Father will be faithful to teach you everything you need to know.* In the verses that follow, seek to know and appreciate your Father more as a loving, patient Teacher.

Identify some of the things the Bible says in these verses about God, your Father, as your Teacher. Exodus 4:12, Psalm 119:26-27, Psalm 144:1, Isaiah

2:3, Isaiah 48:17, Micah 4:2, John 6:45, John 14:26, John 16:13, 2 Corinthians 2:9-12, 1 John 2:27

What are some of the specific things the Bible promises that your heavenly Father will teach you?

Who does Jesus identify as the Agent through whom God teaches those who believe in Him?

Think of some things you can do to make it easier for your Father to teach you what He wants you to know.

Know God as Your Disciplinarian

Hebrews 12:6
For those whom the Lord loves He disciplines, and He scourges every son whom He receives.

Nearly everyone in America is familiar with Dr. James Dobson and his book, *"Dare to Discipline."* On our LIFE TODAY television program we had a series titled, "Parents Who Dared to Discipline." It says something about our society when it takes daring parents to discipline their children. Immediately, it suggests that they are somehow intimidated from performing this parental responsibility. And they certainly are. ***For years many American parents have been deterred from disciplining their children by fear of losing their love or warping their personalities.*** There's also a concern of being reported for child abuse and facing the possibility of arrest and imprisonment for spanking their children, even in their own home!

This trend toward the suppression of parental discipline stems partly from the fact that some parents discipline wrongly and too severely, injuring their children both emotionally and physically. God assuredly frowns on any discipline that is administered selfishly, cruelly or injuriously. ***But He never intended for parents to abandon their disciplinary role in raising their children. Certainly, He disciplines His own children–you, me and all our brothers and sisters in His family.***

Consider the verses that follow, and you will find some thoughts that will help you understand and appreciate God as a loving Father who disciplines His children properly.

In Hebrews 12:4-11, we find many comforting thoughts about our heavenly Father as our Disciplinarian. What thoughts speak to you from the following verses?

Verse 5 _____

_____

Verse 6 _____

_____

Verse 7 _____

_____

Verse 8 _____

_____

Verses 9-10 _____

_____

Verse 11 _____

_____

_____

What do these Old Testament verses reveal about God's motives and purposes in disciplining His children? Job 5:17, Proverbs 3:11-12

Know God as Your Strength

Philippians 4:13
I can do all things through Him who strengthens me.

In your new life in Christ, **you may face problems and challenges that you will not feel you have the strength to handle.** You simply won't be able to deal with them in your human ability. It may be the death of a close loved one. Or a severe physical illness or disability. Or a betrayal by someone you completely trusted. Or a disastrous setback in your career or finances.

Such ordeals are never pleasant for us at the time. But they come sooner or later to almost every Christian—and, as incredible as it seems, God allows them to happen.

Why? Well, that's the question we are all tempted to ask in moments of crisis. And there may be many valid answers. But one answer may be simply that **God wants us to have opportunity to discover and display our Strength.** For He is our Strength.

When you became God's child, you became a being possessing supernatural strength. But if you only faced challenges that could be handled with natural strength, your supernatural abilities would never be revealed. Discover in the following verses how earnestly your Father desires you to know the strength you have in Him.

These verses present many wonderful thoughts concerning the strength your Father provides for you. Identify as many of these thoughts as you can. Philippians 4:13, Psalm 18:1, 29 and 32, Psalm 31:4,

Psalm 59:16-17, Psalm 68:35, Psalm 138:3, Habakkuk 3:19, Colossians 1:11, Ephesians 1:19-20, Ephesians 6:10

Knowing that your Father God is your Strength, will you have a different attitude toward problems that seem beyond your ability to handle? If so, explain the difference it will make.

Know What You Are to God

You can get to know God better as your Father by coming to realize what you are to Him. Consider some of the most exciting things God has made you to be as His child:

You Are His Field and Building

1 Corinthians 3:9
For we are God's fellow workers; you are God's field, God's building.

What thoughts come to your mind when you read this verse identifying Christians as God's field and building? Have you ever thought of yourself this way? **Picturing yourself as God's field, you might see your Father laboring within your own life or among you and your brothers and sisters in Christ.** Seeing yourself as His building, you might envision Him as the Builder, building your life and constructing His church.

What work do you believe your Father is doing in your life and among your fellow Christians?

What work would you like Him to do?

What do you think you might do to speed the work your Father wants to do with you as His field and His building?

You Are His Dwelling

Ephesians 2:22
In whom you also are being built together into a dwelling of God in the Spirit.

Before you received Jesus as Savior and began to know God as Father, you probably thought of God as a Being who lived far away from you. ***Even many Christians, years after being born again, feel there is a great distance between them and their heavenly Father.***

But this is not true. ***God has welcomed us into His very presence through Jesus.*** I suggest that you read Hebrews 4:16 and Hebrews 10:20-22 to see that He invites us to come boldly to Him.

What is still more electrifying, though, is the thought that ***our Father has come to live with us.*** He has made us His dwelling place through His Holy Spirit, who lives in us.

Does knowing that you are your heavenly Father's dwelling place make a difference in how you think about yourself? About how you will live and behave? What specific changes will you make in your life because of this knowledge?

You Are His Friend

John 15:15

No longer do I call you slaves, for the slave does not know what his master is doing; but I have called you friends, for all things that I have heard from My Father I have made known to you.

If you have had an earthly father who was a good provider and protector and who disciplined with love and fairness, you are blessed. **But the best fathers are those, who, in addition to all this, are also good friends to their children.** A good friend is someone who is "there" when you need to talk about things that are bothering you... "there" when you want to share something exciting or celebrate some accomplishment... "there" when you need someone to listen, give you a hug and say, "I understand."

God is just that kind of Father to you. **Through Jesus, He has spoken to all those who believe in Him, saying, "You are my friends."** In the Old Testament, He spoke face to face, as a man talks with his friends, to those who came to Him in faith. You can read about it in Genesis 15:6, Exodus 33:11, Isaiah 41:8 and, in the New Testament, James 2:23.

In what ways does knowing God as your Friend help you to know Him as your Father?

What will you do to get to make your friendship with your heavenly Father more real and more a part of your everyday life?

You Are His Witness

Isaiah 43:12
"It is I who have declared and saved and proclaimed, and there was no stranger {god} among you; so you are My witnesses," declares the Lord, "and I am God."

Some Christians mistakenly think it is their duty to "witness"–to go around accosting people and knocking on doors to tell about Jesus. But **God did not intend us to think of witnessing as a duty.**

I can remember being around a group of kids in school when one of them would say, "Hey, guess what my dad did." And the other kids would be all ears while this boy told how his dad caught a big fish or took him to the circus. Then one of the other boys would pipe up and tell something his dad had done. Not to be outdone, every kid in the group would have to tell something about his or her dad.

Without realizing it, these kids were being witnesses of their fathers. A witness is simply someone who tells what he has seen, heard or experienced. And when you know God as your Father, you will do that. *You won't think of it as a duty. You will be so proud of your Abba Father that you will want to tell everyone you meet everything you know about Him.* Verses like John 15:26-27 and Acts 1:8 say you WILL witness–not that you are commanded.

Since a witness is someone who tells what he has seen and heard, what can you do to be a better witness of your Father?

What do you see as some of the blessings that come with being a faithful witness of your Father?

You Are Part of His Family

Ephesians 2:19
So then you are no longer strangers and aliens, but you are fellow citizens with the saints, and are of God's household.

As I shared in Part I, I got to see how a real father lives and relates to his children during the years I spent with the pastor who took me into his home. After I married and my children came along, I got to experience the joy of being a father myself. Being a father–and grandfather–has helped me more than anything to know God as my Father. But it has taught me something else of great importance: *There is much more to Christianity than just our relationship to our heavenly Father, for when He becomes our Father, we become part of His household, His family.*

Betty and I sometimes just enjoy sitting and watching our children and grandchildren. They are all so beautiful! Our hearts well up with joy when we see them doing things together and enjoying one another. *There is nothing more gratifying, warm and secure than life in a family ruled by love.*

And, of course, God intends His household to be such a family. For His family to be all He designed it to be, however, each member must appreciate all that it means to be part of His family. In the verses that follow, you can learn exciting truths about the privileges that go with being a part of the family of God.

You Have Jesus as Your 'Big Brother'

Hebrews 2:11
For both He who sanctifies and those who are sanctified are all from one Father; for which reason He is not ashamed to call them brethren.

What do the following verses say about Jesus as your Brother? Hebrews 2:11-13 and 17, Romans 8:29, Colossians 1:18

Note some of the implications of the fact that Jesus is your Brother.

To you, what is the most exciting thing about realizing that Jesus is your Brother?

You Share Your Family's Calling

Romans 8:28
And we know that God causes all things to work together for good to those who love God, to those who are called according to His purpose.

What is the meaning of life? Why are we here? Questions like these keep unsaved people bewildered, wandering and unfulfilled. They live out their days with a void in their lives. No degree of success, no amount of money, no height of fame or prestige can ever fill that void because life has no real meaning for them.

For that very reason a wonderful, godly calling is one of the most gratifying aspects of the salvation we receive in Jesus Christ. The Bible says He has a "high calling" for us. There is nothing greater or more noble. Yet it is attainable even for the least of those in the Kingdom of God–because it is guaranteed to us by His promises and His mighty power.

Ultimately, as stated in Romans 8:29, His calling is for us to be conformed to the image of Jesus, God's firstborn Son. *But we are also involved in Christ's entire mission of destroying the works of the devil, setting the captives free and establishing the Kingdom of God in this world.*

We are not to think we must do everything that is in the heart of God, however. Within this great, general calling, *God has specific missions and assignments for each of us individually.* You will experience great joy in discovering, pursuing and fulfilling your part in God's heart! The following verses will help you get started on this fascinating journey.

You may be surprised to learn how much the Bible says about God's calling for your life, now that you are a part of God's family. Carefully consider the content of these verses, for example: Romans 1:6, Romans 9:23-26, 1 Corinthians 1:26-28, Ephesians 1:18, Ephesians 4:1, Ephesians 4:4-6, Colossians 3:15, 2 Thessalonians 2:13-14, 2 Timothy 1:9, Hebrews 9:15, 1 Peter 2:9, 2 Peter 1:3, 2 Peter 1:10, Hebrews 3:1, Jude 1:1

Think about your calling and purpose in connection with the fact that you are part of a family. What part do you believe other members of the family can play in helping you find and fulfill your part in God's heart?

What can you do to help others fulfill their part in God's heart?

You Have a Close Family Fellowship

Romans 12:10-13

Be devoted to one another in brotherly love; give preference to one another in honor; not lagging behind in diligence, fervent in spirit, serving the Lord; rejoicing in hope, persevering in tribulation, devoted to prayer, contributing to the needs of the saints, practicing hospitality.

Of all the blessings my heavenly Father has poured out on me, my family is the one that gives me the greatest joy and satisfaction. A functional family–one that works as God designed families to work–is a beautiful thing to behold. And after years of being denied the experience, I rejoice that I am part of such a family. **Love, of course, is the key. Unconditional love.** God's kind of love. A love in which all know they are accepted on the basis of who they are, not how well they perform. **That kind of love forms the basis for trust–the second requirement of a functional family.** When all individuals know they are accepted and honored, no one has anything to prove. There are no hidden agendas. Everyone can share openly and trust one another without fear of ridicule, scorn or rejection.

In that atmosphere, we weep together when a sorrow comes, rejoice together when good things happen. When a disagreement arises–as is bound to happen in any family–we deal with it by speaking truth in love. We value one another's differences and benefit from them. **Each uses his strengths to support the others in their weaknesses.**

That is how God intends families to operate–including His own family. That is the meaning of fellowship. Now that you are part of His family, your heavenly Father wants you to participate wholeheartedly in its fellowship. In the following verses, let the Spirit make your new family a living reality to you.

What do each of these passages tell you about your heavenly Father's family and how you are to relate to your brothers and sisters in Christ? 1 John 1:3, 1 Corinthians 1:9, Romans 12:15-16, Romans 15:5-6, Ephesians 4:2, Ephesians 5:19-20

What actions and/or attitudes do the above verses suggest for making God's family function as He intends?

Since love is the foundation for a functional family, what can you do to nurture your love for other family members?

What does "forbearance" mean? What things have you already noticed about others in the family of God that call for you to be forbearing toward them?

Your Father's Instructions for Family Living

How can we learn to live as members of the family of God? Well, God did not just create us, tell us to start living as a family and then sit back to see what would happen. He has gone to great lengths to be sure that we know how to live in fellowship with one another as He intends.

First, He has given us an Example. *Jesus Christ, who left heaven to enter the world as a man, lived before us the life God wants us to live.* When we have a question as to how we should relate to another person, all we have to do is look at the life of Jesus.

God has also given us an instruction manual: the Bible. It is filled with directions for living in the family of our heavenly Father. Jesus said to the Father, "Thy word is truth" (John 17:17). That means it is the truth about how we live, as well as about anything else.

He not only has given us instructions, but an Instructor. In John 8:28-29, Jesus let us know that He had an Instructor with Him in the world—God Himself! But in John 16:13, *He tells us that we, too, have an Instructor—the Holy Spirit, the Spirit of God. He lives in us and is always with us, guiding us into all truth.*

Again, a most important part of the truth He shares is simply how to live with one another. And He teaches God's instructions not as law, but as life. The letter kills, but the Spirit gives life (2 Corinthians 3:6).

In the following pages, you will find some of the key instructions our Father has for us in family living.

Love One Another

John 13:34-35
A new commandment I give to you, that you love one another, even as I have loved you, that you also love one another. By this all men will know that you are My disciples, if you have love for one another.

That God desires us to love one another no one can deny. Even those who know little about the Bible have heard that "God is love." **The Bible constantly underlines the importance of carrying out Christ's command to love one another.** Three times it tells us love fulfills God's law (Romans 13:8, Galatians 5:14, James 2:8). It says love covers a multitude of sins (1 Peter 4:8) and that faith does its work through love (Galatians 5:6). It exhorts us to do all that we do through love (1 Corinthians 16:14). It reveals that **the world will know we are disciples of Jesus by our love for one another.** In the following verses, see how many different insights and instructions about love you can find.

John 15:12 and 17, Matthew 5:43-48, Romans 13:8, 1 Thessalonians 3:12, 1 Thessalonians 4:9, 2 Thessalonians 1:3, Hebrews 10:24, 1 Peter 1:22, 1 Peter 4:8, 1 John 3:11 and 23, 1 John 4:7 and 11-12, 2 John 1:5, 1 John 3:16-18

Do you find it hard to love those who are different from you (ethnically, culturally, etc.)? Those who have hurt you? Those who disagree with you? Do you believe you now have the ability to love such people? Can you explain why?

Live in Unity and Harmony

Being diligent to preserve the unity of the Spirit in the bond of peace.

If you have ever experienced family life, you know how important it is for all the members to live together in unity and harmony. ***Bickering and quarreling not only rob the home of peace and joy, but also they undermine the family's strength for dealing with the forces that attack or challenge the family unit.*** Knowing this, Jesus asked the Father to make us all one (John 17:20-21) and warned that a house divided against itself cannot stand (Mark 3:25). ***Paul also admonished believers not to bite and devour one another, lest they utterly consume one another*** (Galatians 5:15).

What thoughts do you see in the following verses concerning the importance of unity in the church, the body of Christ and the family of God? Romans 12:16, Romans 15:5, 1 Corinthians 12:25, Ephesians 4:3 and 25, Philippians 2:2, Acts 1:14, Acts 5:12

What supernatural things happened, according to these three passages, when the first Christians were together and of one mind? Acts 2:46-47, Acts 4:24-31, Acts 5:12

Be Humble

1 Peter 5:5

You younger men, likewise, be subject to your elders; and all of you, clothe yourselves with humility toward one another, for God is opposed to the proud, but gives grace to the humble.

Most people do not like the idea of being humble. In the unsaved person, this is basically because of the rebellious nature inherited from Adam. That nature was born in Adam's refusal to humble himself even before God, his Creator. It detests the thought of being humble before anyone. But, in **Christians, the distaste for the word "humble" may stem from its similarity to another word, "humiliate."** Humiliation indicates unworthiness, shame and degradation. It's important to understand that our **Father does not want us to be humiliated or have a poor self-image.** He wants us to think highly of ourselves–because we are His creation. Yet, at the same time, **He wants us to be humble in the sense of giving ourselves...to Him and to others.**

What do these verses reveal about being humble? Romans 12:3 and 16, Galatians 5:26, Galatians 6:3, Ephesians 4:2, Ephesians 5:21, Colossians 3:12

What two rewards are promised those who humble themselves? 1 Peter 5:4-6

Be Forgiving

Ephesians 4:32
And be kind to one another, tender-hearted, forgiving each other, just as God in Christ also has forgiven you.

You can't read very long in the Bible without coming across the subject of forgiveness. **God places a tremendous emphasis on forgiving.** In His wisdom, He knows that relationships cannot exist without forgiveness. He assures that our own relationship with Him will survive and grow by promising to forgive us. But **He sternly exhorts us to forgive one another.** Only as we obey this command can we live, worship and serve together in peace and power.

What do these verses tell you about forgiving? Matthew 6:12, 14-16; Mark 11:25, Matthew 18:21-35, Luke 17:3-4, Romans 14:13, Galatians 6:1-5, Colossians 3:13, James 4:11, James 5:9

From the above verses, it is clear that God commands us to forgive. But is forgiving easy? Can it be done by mere human power? Or must it be done in dependence on the power of God?

When He was on the cross, who did Jesus turn to in forgiving those who were crucifying Him? Luke 23:34

Do you now have the power to forgive? Explain your answer after reading these verses. John 20:20-23

Encourage Your Brothers and Sisters

1 Thessalonians 5:11
Therefore encourage one another, and build up one another, just as you also are doing.

"Be strong and courageous" and "do not be afraid" are words God often speaks to His people in the Bible. Why does He say this so often? Because *His people–and that includes you now–have an enemy, satan, who is constantly trying to frighten and intimidate us.* Discouragement is one of his most familiar weapons. In His written word and in every way He speaks to us, *our heavenly Father is continually countering the enemy's efforts to discourage us by giving us encouragement. But He also urges His children to encourage one another.* One of the most important services a Christian can perform for other members of the family of God is to lift them up when they are feeling down.

See how many different thoughts you can find about encouragement in the following verses. Romans 1:12, Romans 14:9, Colossians 1:21, Hebrews 3:13, Hebrews 10:25

Think of some things you can do to encourage others when they have been hit by disappointments, failures or setbacks.

On the basis of what you have seen in the above verses, what should you do, as a member of God's family, in times when you are the one who feels discouraged or defeated?

Care for Your Brothers and Sisters

1 John 3:17-18

But whoever has the world's goods, and beholds his brother in need and closes his heart against him, how does the love of God abide in him? Little children, let us not love with word or with tongue, but in deed and truth.

One of the most touching scenes I have ever witnessed unfolded before me on the mission field in Mozambique. We had set up a feeding line to distribute a soup mix to children threatened by starvation. Hundreds of children were lining up, many of them having walked miles to get a bowl of soup. From among all the hungry faces, my eyes singled out a little boy. So weak he could hardly walk, he was half-carrying, half-dragging another child almost his own size. I watched him as he received his soup and found an area where he could sit down to eat it. Then, to my amazement, **using a dried leaf as a spoon, this half-starved boy began to feed the smaller child,** taking a few bites in between for himself. I learned that the smaller child was the boy's little brother.

Our heavenly Father wants us to show that care and concern for our brothers and sisters in the family of God.

What do these verses say about caring for others in your spiritual family? Acts 4:33-35, 1 Corinthians 12:25, Galatians 5:13, Galatians 6:5, Ephesians 4:29,

1 Thessalonians 2:7-11, 1 Thessalonians 5:12-13, 1 Thessalonians 5:15, James 2:15-16, James 5:16

Write down some things you should be prepared to do for brothers and sisters who are in need.

Maintain Unselfish Attitudes

Philippians 2:2-4
Do nothing from selfishness or empty conceit, but with humility of mind let each of you regard one another as more important than himself; do not {merely} look out for your own personal interests, but also for the interests of others.

One of our LIFE TODAY television shows featured a couple specializing in marriage counseling and relationships. At one point I asked them, **"What causes most of the problems you see in relationships?"** Without hesitation, they answered, "Selfishness." A few weeks later, another couple who conduct marriage seminars appeared on the show, and I put the same question to them. The answer came again without hesitation: "Selfishness."

God was so unselfish that He gave His own Son that we might have salvation and come to know Him (John 3:16). And **Jesus was so unselfish that He gave Himself to die on the cross for us** (Ephesians 5:2 and 5:25).

In the following verses, see how many different thoughts you can find about maintaining unselfish attitudes toward your brothers and sisters in Christ. Romans 12:10, Romans 15:7, Colossians 3:9, 1 Thessalonians 5:13, 1 Peter 4:9 and 12, James 3:13-18

According to James 3:15-16, **what happens within our spiritual family when we harbor selfish attitudes?**

Knowing Your Majestic Purpose

Ephesians 1:9-12
He made known to us the mystery of His will, according to His kind intention which He purposed in Him with a view to an administration suitable to the fullness of the times, {that is}, the summing up of all things in Christ, things in the heavens and things upon the earth. In Him also we have obtained an inheritance, having been predestined according to His purpose who works all things after the counsel of His will, to the end that we who were the first to hope in Christ should be to the praise of His glory.

I noted earlier that **one of the greatest problems for the person who does not know God as his Father is finding life's meaning. With God as your Father, however, you have a magnificent purpose. Our Father has placed us in the world to continue and complete the work Jesus Himself began on earth—extending the Kingdom of God to all who will believe.** We are just as He is in the world, 1 John 4:17b says.

What does each of these verses say about His purpose for you? Matthew 6:10, Matthew 28:18-20, Matthew 18:18, Luke 10:17-19, John 14:12-14, 2 Corinthians 10:3-5, 1 Corinthians 6:20, James 5:14-15, Isaiah 58:6-7, 1 John 3:8

Knowing the Holy Spirit Whom God Has Given to Fill You and Anoint Your Life

1 Corinthians 6:19
Do you not know that your body is a temple of the Holy Spirit who is in you, whom you have from God, and that you are not your own?

In John 14:16-18, **Jesus promised that He would not leave us alone in the world** to do the will of God in our own strength and resources. He said He would ask the Father, and **He would send the Holy Spirit to be with us and live in us.** What does each of the following verses say about your relationship with the Holy Spirit? John 20:22, Ephesians 5:18, John 14:26, John 16:13, Romans 8:9, Romans 8:11, Romans 8:13-14, Romans 8:16, 1 Corinthians 2:12, 1 Corinthians 6:19, 1 Corinthians 12:1-12, 1 Thessalonians 2:13, Titus 3:5, 1 John 4:4

The Bible refers to the Holy Spirit by many names. How do His names in these verses help you know and relate to Him? John 14:17, Romans 8:14, Philippians 1:19

Rejoice in Your Wonderful Destiny

With God as your Father and all other born-again believers in Christ as your brothers and sisters, you have a wonderful destiny. *You are a part of God's plan to save and bless not only you, but all people in every nation.* In fact, you will find your greatest blessing in joining hands and hearts with your brothers and sisters to bless others. In Isaiah 61:1-9, the prophet presents a beautiful picture of what God has in store for all His "offspring"–the children He has begotten for Himself through faith in Jesus. *If you have not already become associated with members of your family in the fellowship of a Bible-believing, Spirit-filled church, ask God to lead you to such a congregation.* Then you can join them in worshiping the Lord, praising Him for His goodness and entering into the joyful, fulfilling lifestyle depicted in these verses:

Isaiah 61

1. The Spirit of the Lord God is upon me,
    because the Lord has anointed me
   to bring good news to the afflicted;
   He has sent me to bind up the brokenhearted,
      to proclaim liberty to captives,
   and freedom to prisoners;
2. to proclaim the favorable year of the Lord,
      and the day of vengeance of our God;
   to comfort all who mourn,
3. to grant those who mourn in Zion,
      giving them a garland instead of ashes,
   the oil of gladness instead of mourning,
      the mantel of praise instead of a spirit of fainting.

So they will be called oaks of righteousness,
the planting of the Lord, that He may be glorified.

4. Then they will rebuild the ancient ruins,
they will raise up the former devastations,
and they will repair the ruined cities,
the desolations of many generations.

5. And strangers will stand and pasture your flocks,
and foreigners will be your farmers and your vinedressers.

6. *But you will be called the priests of the Lord;*
you will be spoken of {as} ministers of our God.
You will eat the wealth of nations,
and in their riches you will boast.

7. Instead of your shame
you will have a double portion,
and instead of humiliation
they will shout of joy over their portion.
Therefore, they will possess
a double portion in their land,
everlasting joy will be theirs.

8. For I, the Lord, love justice,
I hate robbery in the burnt offering;
and I will faithfully give them their recompense,
and I will make an everlasting convenant with them.

9. Then their offspring will be known
among the nations,
and their descendants in the midst of the peoples.
All who see them will recognize
them because they are the offspring
whom the Lord has blessed.

In the above passage, I have highlighted some points
that seem important to me. I suggest that you make a
list of the things you find exciting. And, remember,
along with giving you these things to do, God provides
the power, authority and resources to do them!

Finally

You have been given a great invitation: to know God as your Father! As a Christian, you are part of His family and an heir to all that has been promised to Jesus.

Your heavenly Father loves you unconditionally, no matter what. He is an attentive Daddy who is always willing to listen and encourage you. He has forgiven you and cleansed you. He is not keeping a record of your failures, only your victories in Jesus!

Your Father is also full of compassion and wisdom. He wants to help you find your way through life. He knows the questions of your heart and your soul's deepest needs. He sees when you are afraid or lonely, angry, hopeless or despairing, and His heart breaks. He wants you to know His peace and to walk in confidence. He wants to show you His perfect plan for your life and to empower you as never before!

Your Father is a never-ending Source of life, hope, provision and protection. He is a great and mighty Deliverer. He will teach you everything you need to know and correct you when you go astray. He is your Strength when trouble comes, and your Light in the darkness.

You, on the other hand, are His beloved child. You are His fertile field where He plants His Word, His promises, His love. You are His building, the temple of His Holy Spirit. You are a glorious and amazing work in progress!

Your Father has chosen to dwell in your heart. Think of it! He has chosen to live in you and express His character and nature through you. He says you are His friend and asks you to be a witness of His goodness and faithfulness.

God has adopted you and welcomed you into His holy family. He has given you a wise and loving elder Brother, Jesus. He has called you to help fulfill His purposes throughout the earth. He has given you a family that is committed to your growth and success.

He asks you now to live in a way that will bring honor to His name. Love your brothers and sisters in Christ. Live in unity and harmony. Be humble and forgiving. Encourage the downhearted. Care for people. Put others before yourself. Realize you have a great destiny in Jesus. Allow the Holy Spirit to fill you and anoint you for service.

You can enjoy the blessings of your loving heavenly Father today. Why not reach out now and take His hand? As you do, you will begin to see Him more clearly as your Father, and you as His child, and His life will be miraculously expressed through you.

☐ James, after reading your book, I invited Christ into my heart and have accepted God as *my* Father. Please send me additional materials to help me better understand my new relationship with God.

Name _____

Address _____

City_____State ____Zip_____

Phone (_____) _____

☐ Please send me additional information on LIFE Outreach International. (3627)

Fill out this form and send it to LIFE Outreach International, P.O. Box 982000, Fort Worth, Texas 76182, or call (817) 685-5000. In Canada: P.O. Box 4000, Langley, BC V3A 8J8 or call (604) 534-6166.

- -

To order more copies of this book, fill out this form and send it to LIFE Outreach International, P.O. Box 982000, Fort Worth, Texas 76182, or call (817) 685-5000. In Canada: P.O. Box 4000, Langley, BC V3A 8J8. Or visit www.lifetoday.org.

☐ Please send me ____copies of *Knowing God as Father* at $5 each.

Name _____

Address _____

City_____State ____Zip_____

Phone (_____) _____

☐ Please send me additional information on LIFE Outreach International. (3627)

If you or your group would like to order larger quantities of *Knowing God as Father,* please call the offices of LIFE Outreach International for special discounts.

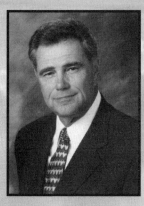

"I want to bring you face-to-face with the perfect Father." – *James Robison*

We all need to know and experience the love of a father. I never did, or so I thought, until I met the perfect Father waiting for me with open arms. That's why I've written this book to show the countless men and women with vague, negative or even non-existent images of a father that God is always there with the unconditional love we all long for in our dads. Find out what the Bible says about our heavenly Father, how to use these fathering traits in your home and family, and how to experience more deeply the love God has for you when you come face-to-face with *My Father's Face.*

James, please send me a copy of your book, *My Father's Face,* for my gift of:_____*

*Suggested donation of $20.

ame: _____Phone: _____

ddress: _____

ity: _____State/Prov.: _____Zip/Postal Code: _____

Please make checks payable to LIFE.
LIFE Outreach International • P.O. Box 982000, Fort Worth, TX 76182
In Canada: P.O. Box 4000, Langley, BC V3A 8J8

16179H